THE PROBLEM WITH ANGER

AND HOW TO SOLVE IT

Also by Roddy Carter

BodyWHealth: Journey to Abundance

Sunset Lessons: Reflections on Light and Love from the Darkest of Places

Fireside Wisdom: Conversations to Inspire Personal Mastery

Unstoppable You Online Courses
(available from www.roddycarter.com):
Unstoppable You
Unstoppable You Business
Unleash Unstoppable
Unleash Success

THE PROBLEM WITH SUFFERING

AND HOW TO SOLVE IT

by Roddy Carter, MD

Illustrated by Hannah Mae Silcock

Aquila Life Science Press
La Jolla, California

FIRST AQUILA LIFE SCIENCE PRESS EDITION, JANUARY 2024
Published by Aquila Life Science, LLC, La Jolla, CA

THE PROBLEM WITH SUFFERING.

ISBN: 978-0-9969889-9-5

Printed in the United States of America

For little Roddy,

and every beautiful,

angry human being,

everywhere.

ACKNOWLEDGEMENTS

This book is about anger. You will soon see that I use my own anger as the portal through which I understand the problem with anger. Before starting the story, I would like to sincerely apologize to all who have suffered my anger. While I am not an excessively angry person, facing anyone's wrath is nevertheless a painful experience. I'm sorry.

I am grateful for life, the greatest of all teachers, who gave me anger in the first place and then invited me to learn about it, and to grow beyond it.

I am deeply indebted to Sarah Dawson, who has edited all my published works. A powerful listener, she understands my voice and works her magic on my stories. She has helped me to capture and translate both fable and science with equal distinction. The life-changing lessons in this book could not have reached you without her. I trust that you will share my appreciation for her remarkable professional talent.

This book is the international debut of artist and illustrator Hannah Silcock. I'm deeply honored to pair my story and guidance with the exquisite creativity of this exceptional young artist. Her illustrations powerfully complement the story of Roddy and his journey with Anger. She has brought magnificent color and depth to my words. I know that you will join me in saluting her genius.

PREFACE

The insight that prompted me to write this book arrived on the morning of my 59th birthday.

"Why not on my 29th birthday?" I asked. "It would have saved me a great deal of pain over the last 30 years."

I can't answer that question.

The insight arrived; that's enough!

If you listen carefully and are willing to do the work, I think that you also may find the insight life changing!

CHAPTER 1

THE STORY OF ANGER

I first met Anger when I was little. And like all little people in the world, I was, well... little!

Actually, I was relatively tall compared with my peers. But in every other way, like every other little person, I was little.

And because I was small, everything and everybody else felt much bigger than me, especially the big people I looked up to.

For the most part, my littleness didn't worry me.

But sometimes, in indescribably scary moments, the big people changed. They seemed to grow and become even bigger than usual. They stood taller. They sometimes waved their arms. They yelled and made loud noises. They stomped and threw things. On occasion, I even saw them reaching out to hurt other people.

This made me scared, and when I got scared,

I felt even smaller.

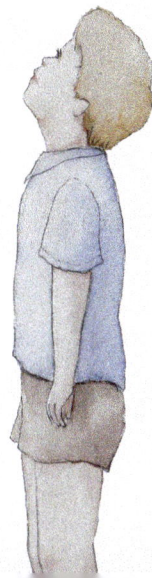

15

Sometimes, some of the older children at school changed like this, too. When that happened, they threatened to hurt me, and I believed they would.

Even my mom, who was loving and kind, would sometimes erupt in this extra-big way. In those moments, when stress and worry invaded her mind, she would charge up the stairs after my fleeing brother and me, wielding a leather sandal threateningly in her hand.

Then there was my language teacher at school. If someone hadn't done their homework or if they spoke without being asked, he would go red in the face, his eyes would bulge, his bony frame would grow until it seemed to block out the light, and he would grab the offending student by the ear, squeezing and twisting it until that little person was in tears.

All these moments made me feel very small...

and

very

afraid.

Then, one day, I found myself frustrated by my little brother.

I was building a model airplane, and I was immersed in its construction with singular focus. As is true for many little brothers, mine was not happy being left out and was pestering me endlessly. I had asked him nicely to stop (several times, actually), but he didn't listen.

Suddenly, something strange happened. Something grew inside of me. It was like a hot, thick liquid that seemed to pulse through my veins and my body.

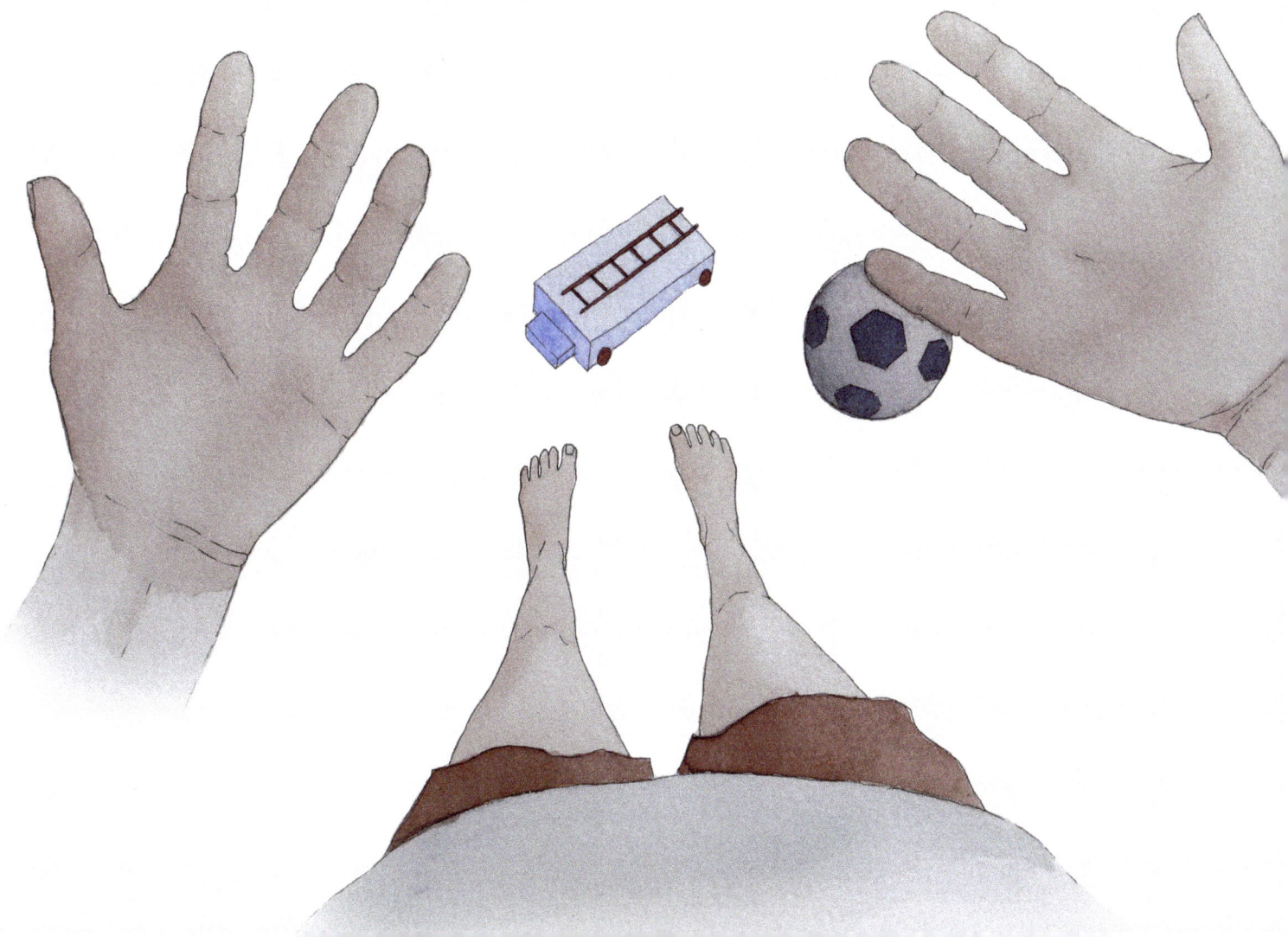

And I grew. I stood taller. I waved my arms around wildly.
My eyes were wide and staring. I shouted with a loud voice.

My little brother shrank away, leaving me in peace and quiet to get on with my big-kid activities.

Wow! Simple!

And the next time my brother pestered me, it happened again. With the same gratifying result.

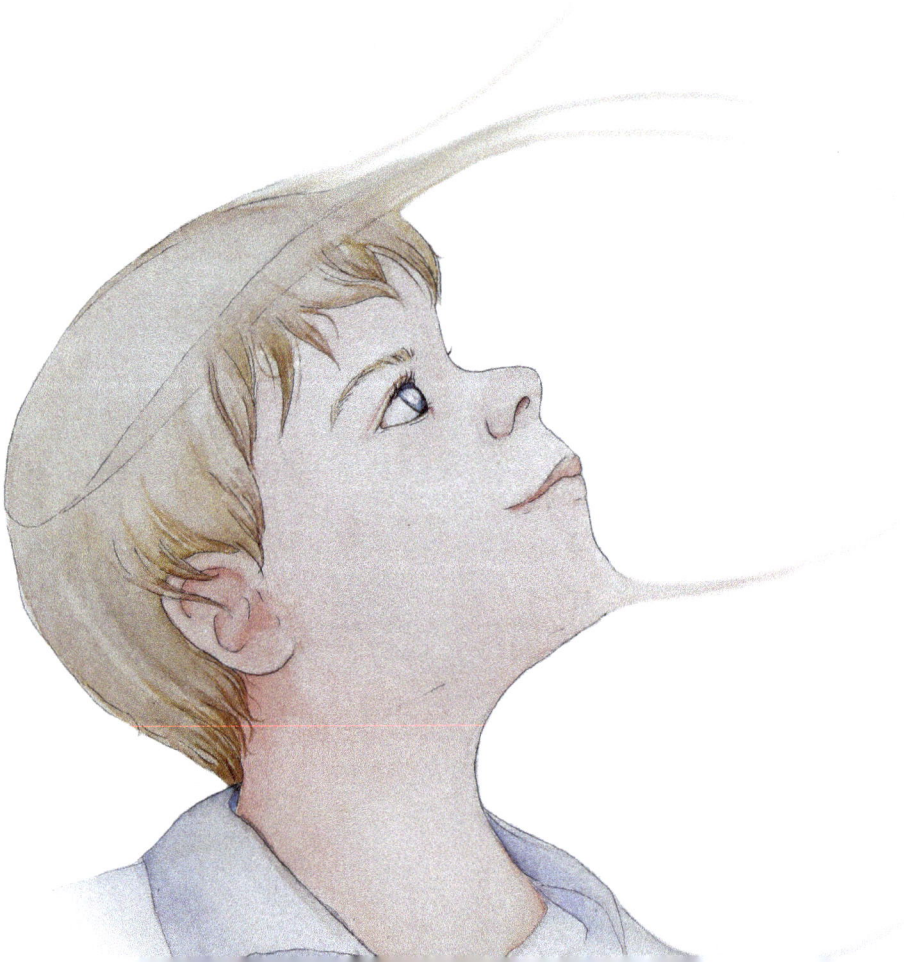

I had found a new friend. His name was Anger.

When he joined me, I felt bigger and got bigger, and things turned out the way I wanted them to be.

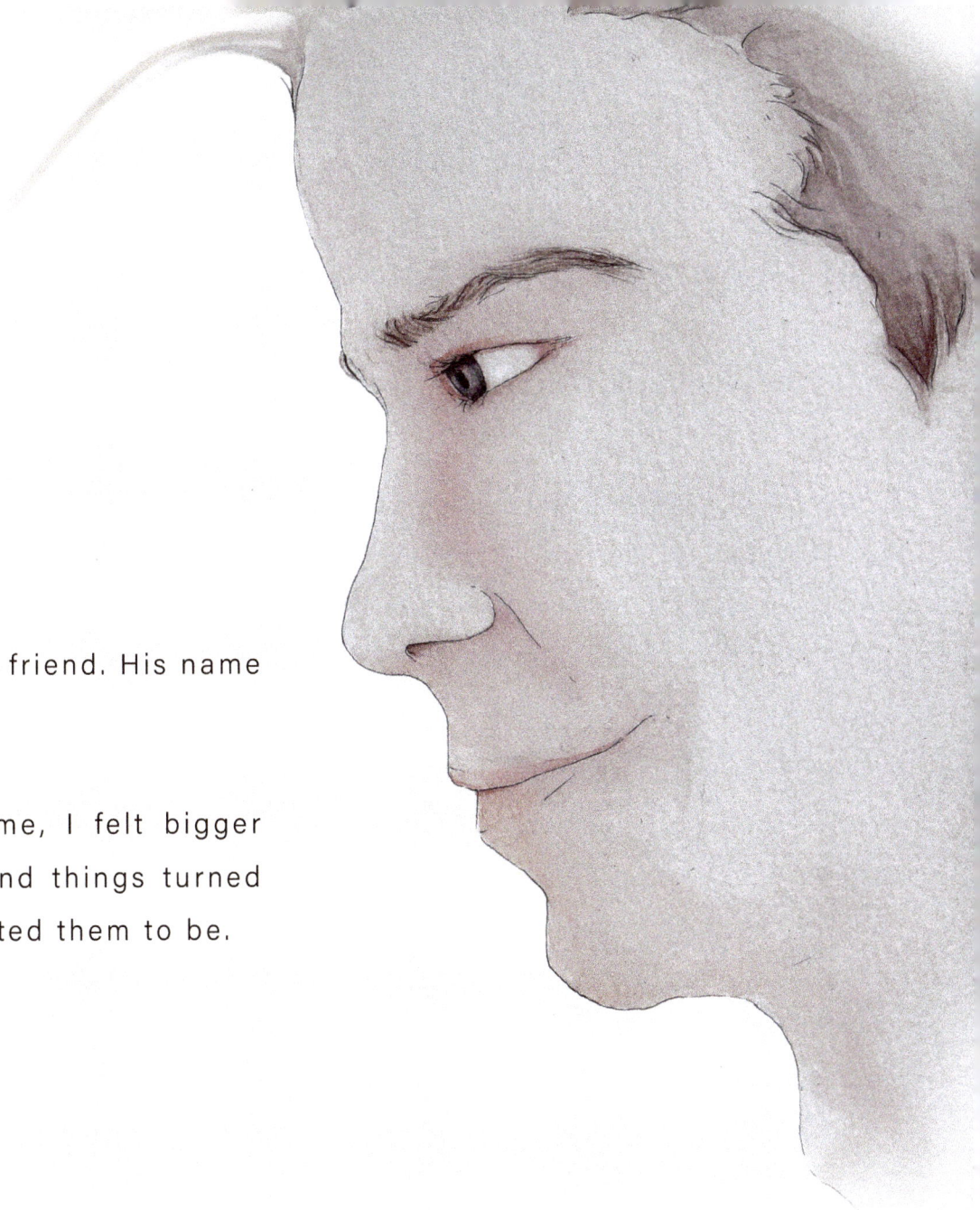

Anger started going to school with me. He helped me on the playground. He protected me from the bullies who had previously pushed me around. More than that, he made me brave enough to help other little people, saving them from the bullies, too.

Anger was a really good guy. He was always willing to step up to help me in tough situations. He was able to make things that were previously scary unscary.

At some point, my parents noticed my new friend. They told me
that Anger wasn't welcome in our house. I tried to listen to them,
but it was hard to argue with the feelings inside...
the feelings of safety and competence...
the bigness that Anger brought
me when he spoke up.

So, I kept him as my friend. I tried to hide him from my family, but I knew that Anger was there whenever I needed him.

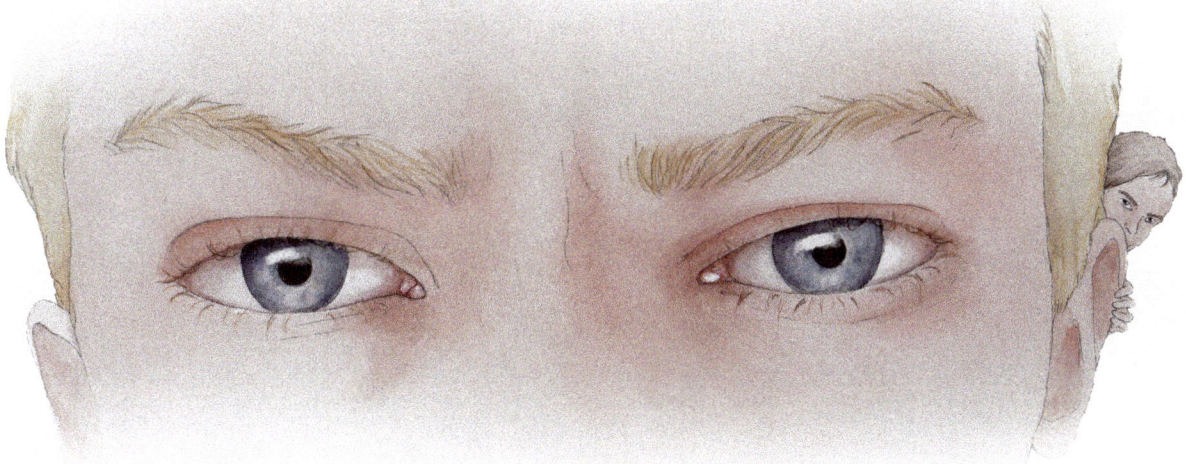

I continued to grow and thrive with my secret new friend at my side.

One day, I became a big person myself. I was so big that it was appropriate for me to find another big person to share my life with. With her, I had four beautiful little people of my own. I also became a caring doctor, and then a scientist, and then a respected business leader.

Through it all, Anger was a loyal friend. He always noticed when problems seemed too big for me. The hot lava would flow in my veins. I would stand extra tall. My eyes would bulge, and my face would go red. I would wave my arms and raise my voice, even at people I loved very much...even at my own little people!

I didn't think about this too much then, but I later realized that it was strange that I needed my friend Anger to inflate me in the presence of my own little people, who were, well, certainly a lot smaller than I was!

I was beginning to notice something important.

There was a problem with my friend, Anger.

Actually, there were many problems.

While Anger sometimes made my problems go away, there were times that he made situations much worse for me, and he sometimes drove me to hurt people.

And I saw how others who also had a friend called Anger
could be very dangerous.

In blind, destructive rage, Anger would lead them to do horrible things. I
watched people under his influence hurt their family and friends, sometimes
physically. Sometimes very badly. Some of them destroyed precious
relationships. Some of them even went to prison.

I also found that Anger encourages Anger. When he made me huge with rage, he often provoked the same behavior in others. They raged, too. These were very ugly, damaging moments between unhappy people trying to be bigger than each other.

As a physician, I learned that Anger was bad for my health. He pushed my blood pressure up. He triggered the release of stress hormones in my body that traveled through my blood to distant organs, where they had nasty, unwanted effects.

Anger clouded my thinking. He made it difficult for me to see peaceful, painless solutions to problems. In these situations, without a clear and simple path forward, I became dependent on Anger. It was quicker and easier to fly into a rage than to navigate the trickier path toward harmonious outcomes.

I also noticed that, after driving me to rage, Anger often woke another friend. That friend's name was Shame. And Shame made me feel terrible—so terrible, in fact, that I didn't feel strong enough to find other solutions to the problems that Anger could fix very quickly and efficiently.

So, as I began to understand the real nature of Anger,
I realized that he had many downsides. But none of those
came at all close to the real problem with Anger.

The real problem with Anger is that

HE

MAKES

ME

FEEL

LITTLE.

That's right! Although I'm a big person now,
when Anger speaks, I feel small again.

When he emerges from the shadows, Anger whispers in
my ear as he did the very first time we met:

"Hello, little boy.
What a sad, weak little person you are.
Let me help you."

"Stand tall, very tall. Lift your arms and wave them
around. Raise your voice into a deafening roar, if
necessary. Do all of this, and you will be bigger than
them. You will be bigger than the problems that are
threatening to crush you."

45

Anger whispers so quietly, and I am so familiar with him, that I don't always notice his undermining influence.

And so, I hear his whispered words every time, without registering or disputing them...and THEY MAKE ME FEEL SMALL.

Sadly, because Anger makes me outwardly large, I completely overlook the fact that, on the inside, where it really matters, he makes me feel small.

And because I feel small, Anger tricks me into thinking that I need him. And so I keep him on as a trusted and loyal helper. I remain trapped, under his spell.

To make matters worse, Anger doesn't only keep me dependent on him by making me feel small.

He guides me to other bad habits, too. Sometimes I put up walls, keeping my love inside me in stony silence and withholding it from those around me. Other times I use my strong intellect to overwhelm other people. Or I tell stories about them behind their backs to undermine them.

I do all these things because Anger makes me feel little.

Even worse, because Anger makes me feel small, I don't trust myself to achieve big things. I don't raise my hand for the next promotion. I set my sights on small goals instead of reaching for the stars. I subtly impair my own performance and success in many unseen ways.

And I'm ashamed to say that, without meaning to, I have suggested this self-defeating strategy to my own little people. They watch me closely, and when they hear the voice of Anger tell me that I'm little, they say, "If Dad is little, and he is so much bigger than I am, then I must be excruciatingly tiny...

I had better find myself a friend called Anger."

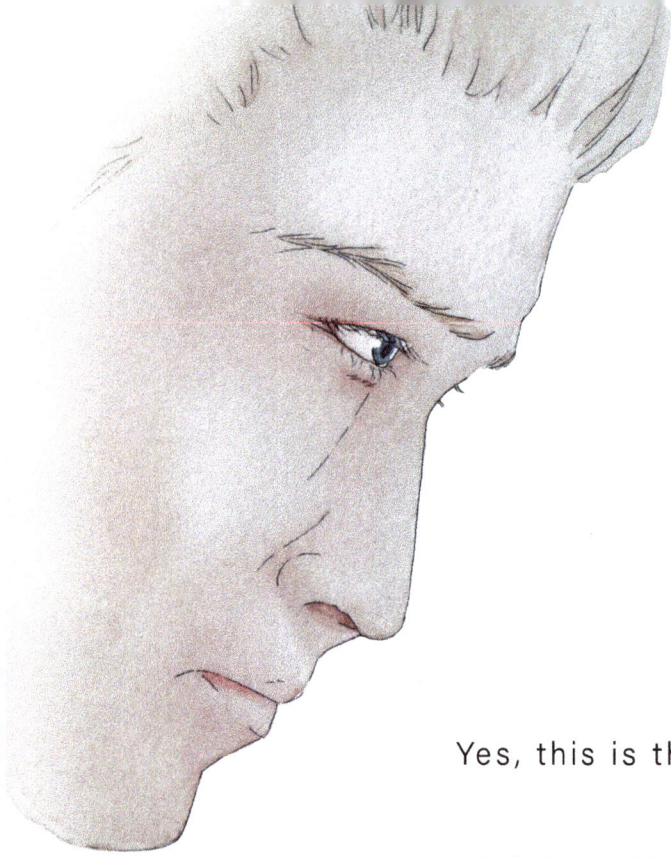

Yes, this is the real problem with Anger:

HE ALWAYS MAKES ME FEEL LITTLE!

Do you have a friend called Anger?

And have you noticed that he or she makes YOU feel little, too?

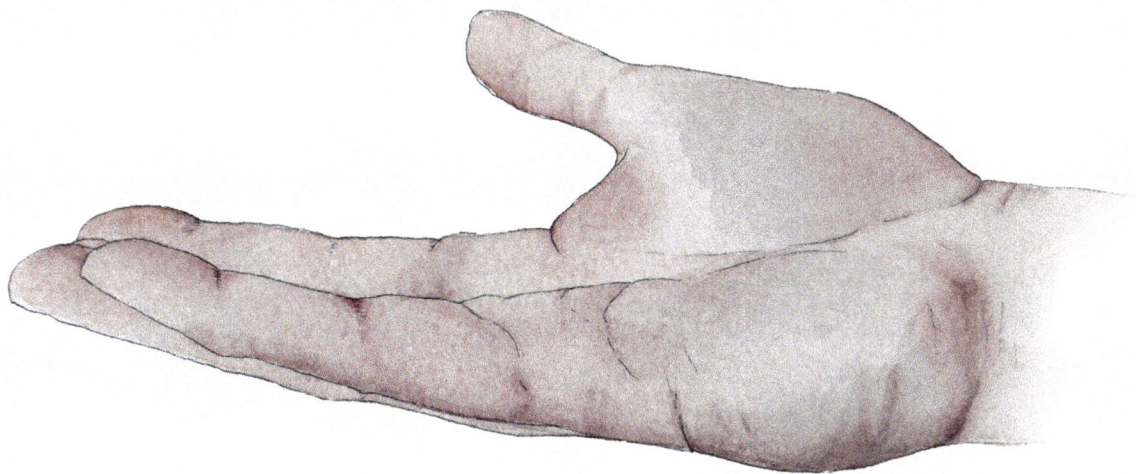

CHAPTER 2

UNDERSTANDING ANGER

I hear you asking me: "Roddy, did you only realize for the first time at the age of 59 that anger was a problem? I can't believe you were not aware of the dangers of this destructive emotion before then!"

Rest assured that I was strongly aware of Anger's destructive influence well before that day. I had seen it graphically impacting many lives around me in both my professional and my personal circles, and I was shamefully aware of its influence in my own life.

In truth, my angry outbursts were moderate in comparison with those of others. But what struck me during the waking hours of that particular birthday was the enormous internal destruction that Anger had wrought upon my psyche, regardless of the modest way his influence translated into outward action.

But this is only half of the birthday story.

To help you understand why this was such a far-reaching realization, I need to give you a little more background information.

You see, the night before, I had woken in the middle of a disturbing dream.

The exact narrative of the dream is immaterial. Suffice it to say that—in the dream—someone I love and care about had "done" something that upset me very much.

You will realize that to say that they had "done something" cannot possibly be correct. They hadn't done anything at all. To the best of my knowledge, they had been sleeping quietly in their own bed, hopefully enjoying happy dreams. So how could they have done anything to upset me?

But, in my dream, they had done something to cause me great pain. And guess what? I woke up angry. Very angry!

Yes, my good friend Anger woke with me, and before I was fully conscious, he had whispered in my ear: "Hello, little boy. I see that so-and-so has offended you, rather badly, actually. Because you are little, you need to stand tall, very tall. Lift your arms and wave them around. Raise your voice into a deafening roar. Do all of this, and you will be bigger than them. You will be bigger than the problems that are threatening to crush you."

Of course, I didn't get up out of bed and wave my arms about; that would have been ridiculous behavior. But Anger was alive and well deep inside me, stirring those profoundly negative emotions. He was about to ruin my day. Had I bought into his ludicrous story, I would have spent my birthday surly and miserable, at the very least.

Luckily—and this was the huge birthday gift—I simply lay there with my eyes closed, contemplating the absurd situation.

Something had happened in my brain while I was asleep. This cerebral electrochemistry had woken my friend Anger—without my permission. Somewhere in the recesses of my sleepy mind, Anger instantly spoke up, and in so doing he *made me feel little*.

And it was this inner message, from a trusted and unquestioned source, that triggered all my negative emotions.

I woke feeling like a pathetic little boy, with limited perspective, hopelessly inadequate problem-solving skills, and insufficient emotional resilience. Feeling small and useless, I started down the destructive behavioral path that a little boy would depend on to solve a problem bigger than he was.

The problem Anger was trying to solve that morning didn't even exist...it was all a totally fictitious, completely invalid construct *in my mind*. During the night, my brain invented a story, and in the morning, my brain reacted with a toxic emotional protection strategy. And I nearly let this ruin my day!

As the sun rose gently into the eastern sky, the problem with Anger became very clear to me: While it may have served me well as a little boy, the anger response is not only a poor problem-solving tool but a deeply undermining and self-destructive response for the intelligent, experienced, and caring adult that I am.

Happy Birthday, Roddy!

HERE TO HELP

Let me explain to you what happened to me that night.

Let me help you understand how you may also have acquired your own friend called Anger.

Let me help you appreciate that this is a part of your normal neurobiology; that you're not broken, but quite okay. Let me help you see that there are ways to work with your brain and your friend Anger, so he stops harming you and so you can stop hurting others, too.

Most of all, let me help you find a new way of relating to yourself, and your friend Anger, so you never again need to feel little—smaller than your biological, cognitive, emotional, or experiential age.

Let me help you find a way to harness your brain in all its immense power to become your friend, and not be your enemy.

My greatest hope is that this message reaches you well before your 59th birthday, and well before you hurt anyone about whom you care (any more than you already have). Most urgently, I hope that you will receive this gift before you train your own children in Anger.

THE PROBLEM WITH ANGER

The story you read in Chapter 1 begins where we all start: when we're little.

It is commonly agreed that humans are the most evolved living organisms on earth, and yet we start our lives useless. After an enormously long gestation period, we must exit the safety of our mother's womb well before our brain is fully developed.

The complex human brain is so large that, were we to be as cognitively advanced as an antelope or horse or dolphin at birth, we simply couldn't make our way through the narrow birth canal. So, we are born useless, before our brain is sufficiently mature, and need many years of neurological development before we are even remotely self-sufficient, never mind valuable to the rest of the species.

Despite this apparent drawback, Nature's design is ideal: We arrive in this world with the perfect inner being.

I have traveled the world and seen children in a wide range of contexts, from the most privileged to the most vulnerable. Across all these different circumstances, one thing always strikes me about children: their innate happiness.

We are born happy.

More than this, we are born kind, courageous, confident, curious, generous, and loving. Deep inside, we all start out as the full package. At birth, we are endowed with the gifts we then spend our adult lives chasing.

But let me quickly remind you that, although we're born inwardly perfect, we're also born outwardly useless.

This is clearly an unsustainable condition. In this state, we need help to simply survive. And survival is indeed our biggest challenge and highest priority.

Once again, Nature comes to the rescue with her ingenious design.

To make us useful, she stretches us. Using a combination of stimuli, she exposes us to situations we have never encountered before, and both with and without adult supervision, we learn what to do. Because these situations are all new to us, they are necessarily stressful—that is, the little challenges are stressful. Bigger ones are downright distressing. Step it up a bit, and the biggest challenges we face are unquestionably traumatic.

Through a combination of stress, distress, and trauma, we are stretched beyond our uselessness toward the sociobiologic competence we refer to as *adulthood*.

Most of this stretching takes place in our neurological system, most particularly in our magnificent brain.

Through a complex process, stress, distress, and trauma invoke adaptive responses in our neurobiology that enable our survival and maturation.

Successful behavioral responses get repeated with sufficient frequency that they become deeply ingrained. Whether we invent the solutions ourselves or copy them from parents and other role models, these adaptive approaches—our biologic algorithms—become substantial new parts of the functional wiring of our developing brains. We become programmed for life.

Today, we increasingly understand the underlying science of this programming that takes place in the human brain. We don't need to explore that in any detail here. It is sufficient for us to know that each algorithm is stored in a series of nerves that wire together in a manner that, when stimulated, triggers a predictable pattern of behavior.

To see this in action, let's go back to the story. Remember little Roddy, who was frustrated by his brother pestering him while he was concentrating on building his model airplane?

One day, either by accident or by copying adult behavior, his brain connected a sequence of nerves that brought about behavior that was totally different from the original Roddy—the cute little boy who had been born a few years previously. On this day, he stood tall, waved his arms, and raised his voice in an aggressive, threatening manner, and his sweet little brother ran away.

And on this day, his friend Anger was born.

I hope that you now understand that Anger is no more than a neurological algorithm, a series of nerves that wire and fire together to produce a distinct, recognizable behavioral output.

And this algorithm was going to produce several problems that lay ahead of little Roddy, which he simply could not have anticipated.

First, because this behavioral strategy worked, he repeated the action again... and again...and again. Anger repeatedly helped him to stop his little brother from pestering him. More than this, little Roddy deployed the new algorithm on the playground to protect himself and other little people from the big bullies. The one-time success became a powerful (and, at the time, useful) default reaction.

Now, wearing my scientist's white coat, I can tell you what was happening in his brain. Each time that little Roddy induced the firing of this specific nerve sequence, the connections between the nerves in this specific conduction chain were selectively strengthening.

Without any algorithmic training, each nerve in the brain can connect directly with a huge number of distal nerves, giving our brain massive computational power. But when a sequence of nerves (in this case, the Anger sequence) fires repeatedly, the connections to specific individual nerves downstream become reinforced. The effect is the creation of deeply rutted highways that make the spontaneous choice of alternative neural pathways less likely.

Anger becomes a default stress response.

And so, each time little Roddy responded to his brother in this way, he fortified his underlying neurobiology, nurturing his new friend Anger, who induced in him a regular, recurring persona that was vastly different from the original and authentic Roddy.

As a second problem, recurring activation of these specific neural pathways bulks them up, like our skeletal muscles when we take them into the gym and strengthen them with resistance training. The nerve enlarges by thickening the insulating layer of fatty material called myelin that surrounds each fiber. The physiological consequence is that these well-trained nerve sequences now fire more rapidly than any other adjacent pathways. The well-rehearsed algorithm operates at lightning speed, much faster than any alternative response.

So, under stress, the brain deploys these default adaptive responses immediately, *even before we can think about it!* Anger becomes an instantaneous and automated stress response to deal with problems—even before we become cognitively aware of the problems.

Third, and most importantly, it appears that the earliest memories associated with each adaptive stress response are stored in close association with the stress response itself. So, when the anger algorithm is activated in adult Roddy, it simultaneously awakens the shadow memories of little Roddy. And when these stress-activated responses were born in little Roddy, he wasn't a happy boy. He was deeply frustrated, even overwhelmed, and didn't know how to solve his problems.

Think of times when you have had your own friend Anger triggered. It's always associated with a miserable, even overwhelming, feeling—a feeling that the problems you're facing in the moment are bigger than you, even though you're a well-developed, intelligent, and experienced adult.

Now you understand why: Because, as your brain instinctively and instantaneously unleashes a protective response, it simultaneously evokes the memory of your useless little self—the frail and fragile little person who was there when Anger was first born. Because of this deeply ingrained neurological association, Anger *makes us feel little*.

This is the problem with Anger.

Anger makes us feel little.

A FAILURE TO NOTICE

There is an additional, longer-term problem within this natural design.

Nature's primary imperative for us is very simple and totally unambiguous: our survival. Every adaptation in our neurobiology is to enhance our survival. If it wasn't, we would all perish as useless little human organisms.

So, Roddy's friend Anger was purely focused on his survival.

What a wonderful friend! He (and a few others) enabled Roddy to survive his early, useless years. Roddy did in fact become a valuable adult. So, we are forever grateful for Anger and his wise early guidance.

But here the model breaks down a bit.

You see, when our brain was originally designed, life was extremely dangerous. Existence was little more than a minute-by-minute survival game. Danger lurked around every corner, with hungry predators and natural competitors waiting for young of every species to make a mistake. A single error could mean death.

And so, at birth, each little newborn hears Nature quietly whisper in their ear.

"Life is dangerous," she says. "I have equipped you with a powerful brain. It comes preprogrammed with algorithms that have enabled your ancestors to survive and to produce you. More than this, it is equipped with exquisitely sensitive surveillance technology that will adopt and adapt any survival strategy that you see deployed around you. And, if this isn't sufficiently impressive, it comes with the innate potential for thoughtfulness. No other living organism has this expansive capacity. Your gifts of thought, reason, memory, and imagination will empower you to supplement these early survival strategies with your own unique adaptations. But, for you to survive, you must first become enslaved to your brain. Your brain must be your supreme commander. You will ignore the directions of your mighty brain at your peril. Let me repeat, little person: If you do not follow the voices you hear within, you will perish."

And because we are useless when we're little, and despite the fact that modern life is considerably safer than historic life, survival remains our highest priority—at first. We are genuinely vulnerable when we're little. We can't feed ourselves or protect ourselves. Without help, our life is at risk.

So, appropriately, we start a life of enslavement to our brain and its survival algorithms.

When Anger was born inside my powerful human supercomputer, and when I heard his voice for the first time, I wisely followed his directions, obediently entrusting him with my survival.

Little Roddy, and every other human being who has reached adulthood—including you, dear Reader—adhered to this primal advice. That's why we became big people. That's how we were able to acquire the maturity, the intellect, and the emotional and physical status we enjoy today.

But, despite you and I growing up, our beautiful brains haven't noticed.

"Really?" you ask. "That's not possible! Surely you're wrong, Roddy. How could this supercomputer, with all its immense power and vast observational skills, not have noticed me growing up?"

To explain this, let me share a real-life story with you.

When I was seventeen years old, a little person came into my life. Beverly was about five when I first met her, the very cute cousin of my future wife.

In due course, I grew up and married Beverly's cousin. We had children. In time, Beverly grew up, too, got married, and had her own children.

One Sunday, we were all sitting together, enjoying the warm afternoon sun in Southern California. At one point, her phone rang, and she stepped away to answer it. It was her travel agent, who had called to confirm their upcoming international vacation.

The unseen speaker must have asked Beverly for her credit card details. Obligingly, she read them out into her mobile phone.

This stopped me in my tracks. *What?!* I yelled inside my head. *Beverly, what are you doing?! You're not old enough to have a credit card! No, hold on! You're not even old enough to be traveling...to be married...to have children.*

Whoa! What is going on here?

You see, I had Beverly fixed in my mind as a cute little five-year-old, suspended in my brain's electrochemistry exactly as she had been when I first met her. I know that you've had this experience, too. We all have. You too have seen somebody after a long time and been shocked at how they have grown up, or grown old.

In this moment, I had a sudden and shocking realization: If my powerful brain had frozen Beverly at the age and stage she was when I first met her, then why wouldn't it do the same with me?

I instantly recognized that my own brain had frozen me, and now repeatedly remembered me, at the age and stage I had been when it first became aware of me—as little Roddy.

My friend Anger met me as a weak (because I was young), resourceless (because I was young), and vulnerable (because I was young) little boy. And so, he lovingly jumped into action to protect me.

And this is how Anger still sees me!

Despite me growing up—despite me now being a strong, robust, and resourceful adult—Anger still sees me as a little boy, and with the very best of intentions continues to advise me to stand tall, to lift my arms and wave them wildly in the air, and to raise my voice in a deafening roar to make me appear bigger than them, bigger than any problem that threatens me. And he does this by referring to the mental image frozen deep within my mind of weak little Roddy.

Without knowing it, Beverly taught me how and why Anger hurts me, and you, and every one of us who has ever been guided by him.

CHAPTER 3

_____

TAMING ANGER

At some point in the life of every human being, I believe we get a wake-up call.

I call this *the Invitation*.

It often comes after a great disaster, or collapse, or misadventure. In her book *Daring Greatly*, Brené Brown refers to this as the moment we awaken face-down in the arena, invoking images of gladiators who have ferociously competed (in the game of life) and come unstuck.

In this glorious moment, we receive a lifesaving call. For some, it sounds like a raucous bugle calling us to our senses at the crack of dawn. For others, it may be a barely audible whisper—so soft they may even doubt its existence.

Either way, the Invitation comes, encouraging us to go within, to understand who we are and how we came to be who we are. It awakens the dormant memory of the good life, the beautiful, happy, trusting, curious, and confident little us who first arrived on this earth. It allures us with the possibility of regaining this highly desirable state. And, most importantly, it brings us the shocking news that, contrary to the early survival-based enslavement mandate, our magnificent brain was given to us as a gift to use—a powerful tool to entrain and harness—to move toward the life of our dreams. The Invitation gifts us with the realization that the human brain, like every other organ we have, is here to serve us in our adult life, and not vice versa.

When I—a serious and committed Western scientist—realized this, I was flabbergasted. They didn't teach me this in medical school.

To be honest, I was also a little embarrassed, even ashamed. I felt stupid for enslaving myself to my own brain, to Anger and all his friends.

Over time, I have learned to appreciate all these survival algorithms, including Anger. After all, they kept me safe, enabling my maturation. In unseen and thankless ways throughout my early life, they valiantly, with love and devotion, stepped up to protect me, to ensure my survival, and to guide me into adulthood.

Our initial algorithms are designed for us to survive, but not to thrive. To thrive, we need to explore, understand, and deconstruct our fundamental neurobiology. We need to show our brains that we have grown up. We need to modify the foundational structure and function of our magnificent brains, detraining default survival pathways, slowing them down, and enabling the voluntary selection of new strategies for thriving.

Fortunately, this is possible. One of the greatest discoveries of our generation is that our brain is malleable; we can change it. When I was trained as a physician, we were taught that the adult human brain is fully formed and static. If we lost part of it to injury, that was too bad—the function associated with that part was gone forever. But no more! Today, we know that we can substantially remodel the adult human brain. This capacity has been termed *neuroplasticity*.

As a result of neuroplasticity, each of us can respond affirmatively to the Invitation. Each of us can identify and appraise the algorithms that have brought us (as slaves) into adulthood. More importantly, we can retrain and rewire our brains to work for us. We are invited to harness our brains, invoking new strategies for thriving, invoking a gift I refer to as *personal mastery*.

We are able to overcome the primary problem with Anger, avoiding the ongoing and deeply destructive belittlement that we feel as a result of his influence.

So, how do we do this? How do we tame Anger?

It all starts with awareness. Once we understand our underlying neurobiology, we can modify it. Once we have learned how the computer is programmed, we can reprogram it.

So, start with a pause.

You know the advice to count to ten when you're feeling overwhelmed? This is its value: When you pause, you become aware of the things happening inside your head that are so familiar you don't even notice them anymore.

Listen for the voice of Anger.

At first, you probably won't hear any voice. But you will recognize the emotion, for sure—anything from feeling mildly irritated or cold and distant to being consumed by the "red mist." Your own flavors of anger will be intensely familiar to you.

But what I recommend is for you to enter the theatre of your imagination, and to listen very carefully for the voice that speaks behind the emotion. This is your friend

Anger. You will hear him telling you that you are little, useless, and overwhelmed. And because the voice comes from deep within, you believe it and instantly end up feeling little and useless and overwhelmed. And so, you are willing to follow Anger's advice.

Using the power of our imagination, we can see Anger for what he is. Rather than identifying with him (thinking we *are* him), we remember that he is only a survival-based algorithm for little people. When we are not entrapped by his words, we notice that we aren't little anymore and don't need to follow his (bad) advice. We have a choice in the matter and can now exercise that choice in exploring alternative strategies for solving what may still be real problems.

But it will take time and practice.

The memory of your little self is deeply ingrained, like my memory of little Beverly. The deeply rutted nerve highways are resistant to change. The reinforcing neurophysiology needs to be actively countered over and over again. Just like hypertrophied muscles, we need to stop exercising them before they start shrinking.

So, we must remain vigilant for the voice and actions of our friend Anger.

Remember that frequent neurological responses become automated. They disappear into our subconscious, even unconscious.

You have surely driven home on autopilot sometimes, getting to your front door and realizing that you negotiated seven traffic lights on the way but don't remember a single intersection; you can only hope that you obeyed the signals and only crossed when the lights were green! Because driving home is a frequent occurrence, you have automated the process, relegating it to your subconscious.

So too with Anger; the frequency with which we have succumbed to his control has compromised our awareness of him. Our brain has moved him into the background. We have relegated him into our subconscious.

We need to bring his automated sequence into our conscious mind. We need to be aware of when he taps us on the shoulder with his anachronistic advice. We need to stand resolute in our self-awareness as a big person, refuting his assertions and ignoring his recommendations.

We need to reeducate Anger.

Each time he appears lovingly at our side, ready to help us, we need to remind him to look carefully at us; to show him that we have indeed grown up. We need to graphically illuminate our current age and competence for Anger to see.

Here we find mantras helpful. We can repeat positive statements like "I am a full-grown, competent adult" or "I have the mental capacity and emotional depth now to solve big problems calmly and rationally."

The good thing is that our brain eventually notices that Anger is expensive. He consumes mental and emotional energy, unnecessarily. Another of Nature's founding principles is energy conservation, so, when our powerful brain realizes that it is wasting energy in destructive responses, it avoids them. Our friend Anger is now discouraged by the same natural forces that gave rise to him in the first place.

Gradually, working hard on a daily basis, you can get Anger to step down. When we no longer need his help, he doesn't fire as often. Neurologically, the ruts in the highway become shallower and the nerve sequence fires less rapidly, allowing you to think before you react.

You now hold authority over Anger, as opposed to the other way around.

CHAPTER 4

A LIFE OF PEACE AND JOY

This book is not intended to be a comprehensive coaching manual for people needing anger management. Instead, it is my intention to share a colorful and readily digestible translation of the complex neurobiology that results in anger, and more specifically its self-perpetuating, self-destructive nature.

I hope that the insights and knowledge you gained in reading this book inspire your onward journey.

Achieving ideal consciousness is a process, occurring in four stages: *Unconscious Disintegration*, *Conscious Disintegration*, *Conscious Integration*, and *Unconscious Integration*. Each layer of the onion we peel back brings us closer to our original, authentic SELF...that primal being who entered the world in a state of beautifully integrated joy, confidence, curiosity, trust, generosity, kindness, and love.

Survival demands neuropsychological adaptation, and so following our birth we quickly enter the phase of Unconscious Disintegration, in which our brains lead us forward to dis-integrate our SELF using default survival algorithms and their deeply engraved neural pathways. In this phase, we are appropriately focused solely on survival and are not aware that we don't yet know how to live more authentically.

At some point, after establishing very solid survival-based lives, we hear the invitation to bring these automated responses into our awareness (the phase of Conscious Disintegration). If we accept the invitation, we soon learn that something isn't working for us, even as it continues to interfere with our optimal performance.

Anger is not our only survival-based brain algorithm. I believe we each have as many small inner contributors as we have the patience to listen for. Not surprisingly, given their origination at a time when we were little, each of them in their own unique way causes us to feel little—overwhelmed, less than, inadequate. You have, no doubt, heard of "imposter syndrome," the persistence of feelings of inadequacy despite evidence to the contrary. You now know where it comes from.

Today I work with senior leaders—highly successful members of our community—to help them identify the unique portfolio of deep algorithms that stand in their way, keeping them from the full success they deserve.

With the appropriate insight and tools, and as long as we understand that each of these attitude-behavior patterns is just an algorithm that lives and acts through the complex electrophysiology of our beautiful brain, programmed when we were little and needed help, even protection...

we can change.

We can evaluate the algorithms that are working for us, and those that no longer serve us.

We can intervene, entering the phase of Conscious Integration. As we take the appropriate actions, the power these algorithms hold over us begins to decay. As each of these voices starts to atrophy, so too does their destructive influence—and we can begin to return to the beautifully integrated SELF we were at birth.

This early work requires great dedication. Luckily, the process of deliberate detraining is effective, and we can systematically regain authority over our magnificent brain.

In the fantastic final step, we enter the very pleasant phase of Unconscious Integration. We again automate our success, and healthier algorithms become our default responses to future challenges. Our reprogrammed and rewired brain works quietly and seamlessly in the background. We act with a new, peaceful, and positive instinct, without having to think about the best course of action to pursue.

Each successive step of our great journey takes us back toward our authentic SELF, restoring the peace and joy that is our natural birthright.

¤ ¤ ¤ ¤ ¤

Before we drop the curtain on the theatre of our imaginations, let's return to the story we started with.

Please join me in celebrating a more conscious Roddy, who is now more aware, acutely vigilant in listening for the damning voice that once whispered in his ears, "Hello, little boy."

Each time I master such a voice, I start to realize, deep inside, that I am no longer a little boy.

Please join me on this journey. You too can identify and reeducate survival algorithms that served you well in your childhood but now stand in your way, diminishing your confidence and obscuring the clarity with which you deserve to see the world.

When we identify and gain authority over our survival algorithms, we evolve; we advance meaningfully on our journey toward ideal consciousness. With each step, we gain more complete access to the perfect blueprint with which we each started our mortal journey: the blueprint for a life of peace and joy.

CONNECT

You can visit me at my website, www.RoddyCarter.com. There, you will find more of my work that is designed to help you on your journey of conscious living, along with my recommendations for additional reading and research. Please reach out to me directly at connect@RoddyCarter.com to share your victories and struggles.

> If this book resonated with you, I'd be honored if you'd leave a review on the site where you purchased it...your voice helps others find it.

www.ingramcontent.com/pod-product-compliance
Lightning Source LLC
Chambersburg PA
CBHW060752150426
42811CB00058B/1385